FINANCIAL STATEMENTS ANALYSIS

Toye Adelaja

FINANCIAL STATEMENTS ANALYSIS

Copyright © 2015 by (Toye Adelaja)

ISBN 978- 1512197662

Table of Contents

CHAPTER ONE

FINANCIAL STATEMENTS

1.1 Financial Information

Financial information is the basis for financial analysis. Financial information is used by many users of accounting information to predict and evaluate financial performance and financial position of a business entity. Financial information of a company is contained in its financial statements.

1.2 Financial Statements

Financial statements are the reports produced by a business entity to show its financial activities for a particular period of time. Financial statements show the over all operation of the business for each accounting year. Financial statements are the written reports that show how the resources of business owners, creditors and lenders to the business are being utilized to generate income. Financial statements can also be defined as written reports that reflect the strength, weakness and liquidity of a business entity.

Financial statements are prepared from the accounting records and books kept by a business entity. Generally Accepted Accounting Principles and procedures, and International Financial Reporting Standards are applied in preparing the statements.

1.3 Objectives of Financial Statements

The primary objective of financial statements is for the purpose of decision making.
The secondary objectives are as follows:
  a. They provide information that can be used to compute future earnings of the business.
  b. They provide information that shows financial performance and position of a business entity,

1.4 Types of Financial Statements

Financial statements can be classified into 4 main types. They are:
1. Statement of financial position
2. Statement of comprehensive income
3. Statement of cash flow
4. Statement of changes in equity

1.4.1 Statement of Financial Position

Statement of financial position, also known as balance sheet shows the financial position of an entity at a particular period of time. It is divided into 3 segments or elements namely assets, liabilities and equities.

Assets are the resources or property which a business entity own or control. Assets can also be defined as resources controlled by an enterprise as a result of past event from which future economy benefits are expected to flow to the entity. Assets can be divided into non-current assets and current assets. Examples of assets are machinery, land and buildings, computer systems, Goodwill, copy right, cash, bank balance, inventory etc.

Liabilities are the total funds owed for the assets supplied to a business or expenses incurred by a business but not yet paid. Liabilities can be classified into non-current liabilities and current liabilities. Examples of liabilities are debenture, loan stock, bank loans, trade creditors, accrual expenses etc.

Equities can also be referred to as capital of the owner of the business. They are the funds invested into the business.

Functions of Statement of Financial Position

The following are the functions of financial statements:
1. It shows a precise summary of a company's resources and obligations
2. It reflects information about a company's solvency and liquidity.

1.4.2. Statement of Comprehensive Income

Statement of a comprehensive income shows the performance of a business for an accounting period. Elements of the statement of comprehensive income are as follows:

Revenue: Revenue is another name for sales. It is the amount of money received or receivable for the sales of goods or services of a business entity.

Expenses: Expenses are the overhead cost or money spent for the operation of the business. Examples are cost of fuel and lubricants, salary and wages, rent, insurance etc.

Other income: income such as discounts received, commission received etc are categorized as income.

The major purpose of comprehensive income is to show information about the profitability of a business entity.

1.4.3. Statement of Cash Flow

Statement of cash flow is a statement that shows how funds are generated and how they are being utilized. The elements of cash flow are:
1. Cash flow from operating activities
2. Cash flow from investing activities
3. Cash flow from financing activities

1.4.4. Statement of Changes in Equities

Statement of changes in equities is a statement that reports how the profits available to shareholders are being distributed.

Some elements of statement of changes in equities are as follows:
1. Transfer to reserves
2. Preferred stock dividend
3. Common stock dividend
4. Retained earnings

CHAPTER TWO

ANALYSIS OF FINANCIAL STATEMENT

Financial statement analysis is the process of reviewing, evaluating and analyzing the financial statement of a business entity, thereby gaining more understanding of the financial strength and weakness of the business. Financial statement analysis can also be defined as the evaluation and analysis of a company's financial statement to make better economic decision.

Users of financial information can get further insight about the financial health of a company if they properly analyze information provided in the financial statements.

2.1.Users of Financial/Accounting Information
Users of financial/accounting information are as follows:
1. Owners or Shareholders
2. Tax Authority
3. Employees
4. Trade Creditors
5. Banks and other Lending Institutions
6. Creditors and Debtors
7. Competitors
8. Prospective buyers
9. Management

Users of accounting information can be classified into internal users (primary users) and external users (secondary users). The following are the basic explanations of the uses of accounting information to the users:

Internal users include the following:
❖ Owners: To determine the profitability and viability of their investment in a business entity
❖ Employees: for assessing the ability of a company to pay increment in salary, retirement benefits and pensions. They

also use it to assess the financial stability of a company and job security.

❖ Management: They use it for decision making.

External users include the following:

❖ Potential Investors: They use it to determine the earning power of a company they are planning to invest in.

❖ Trade Creditors: They use it to assess the ability of a company to meet its financial obligation as at when due.

❖ Customers : They use it to evaluate the financial stability and the ability of a company to maintain continuous supply of goods

❖ Tax Authority: It is used for the calculation of tax liability of a company filing a tax return.

❖ Competitors: They use it for comparing their financial performances with another company.

❖ Banks and other Lending Institutions: They need it to assess the ability of a company to pay back both interests on loans and principal loans

CHAPTER THREE

FINANCIAL ANALYSIS USING RATIOS AS TOOLS

3.1.   Ratio

Ratio is used as a yardstick for evaluating the financial performance and financial position of a company.

The absolute accounting figures recorded in the financial statements cannot provide meaningful understanding of the performance and position of a business entity.

The relationship between two accounting figures expressed mathematically is known as Financial Ratio or Accounting Ratio.

Ratio makes it possible for users of financial information to get more understanding about the financial strength and weakness of a business entity.

3.2.   Types of Financial analysis

There are many types of financial analysis. They are as follows:

1. Time series analysis: This is the method of analyzing the performance of a company by comparing the present ratio with the past ratio.
2. Industrial analysis: This is the comparison of a company ratio with the average industrial ratio fixed for all the companies operating in the industry.
3. Cross sectional analysis: This involves comparing the ratios of one company with some selected companies in the same industry at the same point in time.
4. Pro-forma analysis: This is the comparison of a ratio calculated from the financial information of a company with a projected ratio set by the company.

CHAPTER FOUR

FINANCIAL ACTIVITIES/RATIOS

4.1. Types of Financial Activities/Ratio

The types of accounting ratios to be calculated are based on the intending uses of financial information. The following are the types of financial activities/accounting ratio:
   a. Profitability ratios and Efficiency ratio
   b. Liquidity ratio or short-term solvency ratio
   c. Long-term solvency or debt ratio
   d. Shareholders investment Ratios

4.1.1   Profitability Ratio and Efficiency ratio

Profitability ratio measures the performance of a business through profits. It is the ratio that is used to evaluate and access business ability to generate earnings having taken into consideration expenses incurred by the business. The higher the profitability ratio of a company, the more profitable the company is.

Efficiency ratio is the ratio that is used to measure how efficient the assets of a company are being utilized to generate profit. A major efficiency ratio is asset turnover ratio.

The common types of profitability ratio are as follows:
1. Gross profit margin
2. Net profit margin
3. Operating expenses ratio
4. Return on capital employed (ROCE)
5. Asset turnover ratio

4.1.2.   Liquidity Ratio

Liquidity ratio is a financial ratio that is used to test a company's ability to meet and settle its short-term financial obligation as at when due.

A company should ensure that it does not suffer from lack of liquidity and does not keep excess funds. The inability of a company to meet its short-term financial obligations due to lack of sufficient liquidity will result in a poor credit worthiness, loss of creditors' confidence or even folding up of the company. A very high liquidity ratio is not good because idle asset will earn nothing.

The following are the various liquidity ratios:

1. Quick Ratio or Acid test Ratio
2. Current Asset Ratio
3. Cash Ratio
4. Stock Turnover Ratio
5. Accounts Receivable Collection Period
6. Accounts Payable Payment Period

4.1.3. Long –Term Solvency or Debt Ratio

Long-term solvency ratio measures the company's ability to meet its long-term financial obligation as at when due.

Long-term solvency ratios may be calculated from statements of financial position items to determine the proportion of debts in total financing. Long-term solvency ratios are also computed from statements of comprehensive income by determining the extent to which operating profit are sufficient to cover fixed charges.

Examples of long-term solvency ratio are:
a. Debt ratio
b. Gearing ratio
c. Interest cover ratio
d. Proprietary ratio
e. Cash flow ratio

4.1.4. Shareholders investment ratio

These are the accounting ratios which help equity shareholders and other investors to evaluate the quality and value of an investment in common stock of a company. The worth or value of an investment in common stock in a quoted company is its market value.

Shareholders' investment ratios are as follows:
a. Earnings per share
b. Earnings yield
c. Dividend per share
d. Dividend cover
e. Dividend yield
f. P/E Ratio

4.2. Standard of Comparison of Ratio for the Purpose of Financial Statement analysis

A single ratio is not meaningful enough to take decision because it is meaningless. One ratio cannot be compared with itself. A single ratio, in itself cannot be used to determine the financial strength or weakness of a business. It should be compared with some standards.

The following are the standards of comparison:
1. Past ratios: These are ratios calculated from past financial statements of a company.
2. Projected ratios are the ratios computed using projected financial statements of the company.
3. Industry ratios: These are the ratios of the industry to which the company operates and belongs
4. Competitors' ratios: These are the ratios of some chosen companies especially the progressive competitors which are in the same industry as the company under consideration.

CHAPTER FIVE

Computation of Investment Ratios

Investment ratios are used by shareholders and other investors to evaluate the performance of a business and to know the value of their investment in stocks of a company

The following were extracted from the statement of changes in equity of Jendo International Ltd.

	2014	2013
	$	$
Net profit after taxation	24,960	21,940
Dividend proposed	-12,000	-11,500
Retained profit	12,960	10,440

An extract from the statements of financial position as at 31st December, 2014

	2014	2013
	$	$
Common stock of $1 each	50,000	42,000
Share premium	18,000	18,000
Capital reserve	22,000	22,000
Revenue reserve	32,000	25,000
	122,000	107,000
Non-current liabilities		
10% debenture	15,000	15,000
	137,000	122,000

NOTE: The market price of the company's share has been fairly stable at $4 per share.

Taxation for year 2014 and 2013 were $10,697 and $9,403 respectively.

Past ratios are used as the basis of comparison for the purpose of the following activities/stockholders' investment ratio.

Calculate the following investment ratios and make necessary interpretation

i.   earnings per share
ii.   dividend per share
iii.   dividend yield
iv.   earnings yield
v.   dividend cover
vi.   Price/Earnings ratio

SOLUTION
i.

	2014	2013

$$EPS = \frac{\text{Net profit after tax and preference dividend}}{\text{Numbers of ordinary shares}}$$

EPS =	$\frac{\$24,960}{50,000}$	$\frac{\$21,940}{42,000}$
EPS =	$0.50	$0.52

Note: EPS = earnings per shares
       : Net profit after tax and preferred dividend is the profit available to common stockholder for distribution.

Earnings per share fell from $0.522 in year 2013 to $0.499 in year 2014. This shows that the performance of the company was better in year 2013 than year 2014.

ii.

The profit available to common stockholders are the profit after tax but the amount that they received is the amount distributed as dividend.

Dividend per share is a ratio that is used to evaluate the total amount of dividend payable per share issued. Therefore dividend per share can be calculated as follow:

		2014	2013
Divided per share			
=	Divided		
	Number of shares		
		$12,000	$11,500
=		50,000	42,000
=		$0.24	$0.27

The dividend decreased in year 2014 by $0.034 i.e. $(0.272 – 0.24). This reduction in dividend per share may discourage investors and make them to invest their funds somewhere else.

There are other two ratios that should be calculated when dividend per share is related to earnings per share. They are as follows:

a. Dividend cover = $\dfrac{\text{Earnings per share}}{\text{Dividend per share}}$

b. Dividend payout ratio is the reciprocal of dividend cover. It is calculated as follows:

Dividend payout ratio = $\dfrac{\text{Dividend per share}}{\text{Earnings per share}}$

iii.

Dividend yield is the return a stockholder is currently expecting on the stock of a company.

Dividend yield =
$$\frac{\text{Dividend per share}}{\text{Market price per share}} \times \frac{100}{1}$$

$$\frac{\$0.24}{\$4} \times 100 \qquad\qquad \frac{\$0.274}{\$4} \times 100$$
$$= 6\% \qquad\qquad = 6.85\%$$

The dividend yield for year 2014 was 6% and the dividend yield in year 2013 was 6.85%. Investors had better opportunity as regard dividend in year 2013 than in year 2014.

iv. Earnings yield evaluate the stockholders' return in relation to the market value of the shares

Earnings yield $= \dfrac{\text{Earnings per share}}{\text{Market price per share}} \times 100$

$$\frac{\$0.499}{\$4} \times 100 \qquad\qquad = \frac{\$0.522}{\$4} \times 100$$

$$= 12.48\% \qquad\qquad = 13.05\%$$

v.

Divided cover ratio measures the number of times in which the earnings available to common stockholders will be able to pay dividend declared.

Dividend cover $= \dfrac{\text{Earnings per share}}{\text{Dividend per share}}$

$$= \quad \$0.499 \qquad\qquad = \quad \$0.522$$

$$\begin{array}{ll} = \dfrac{\$0.24}{2.08\text{times}} & = \dfrac{\$0.274}{1.91\text{times}} \end{array}$$

The dividend cover for the year 2014 was 2.08times while that of 2013 was 1.91times. It showed that the investors and stockholders will be more beneficial in year 2014 than in year 2013.

vi.

Price/ Earnings ratio is the ratio that compares the current share price of a company to its earnings per share.

Price earnings ratio is the price an investor is paying for $1 of a company's earnings or profit. It is the reciprocal of earnings yield.

A high price earnings ratio shows that investors are expecting a higher earnings growth in the future compared to companies with lower price earnings ratio.

Price/Earnings ratio = $\dfrac{\text{Market price per share}}{\text{Earnings per share}}$

$$\begin{array}{ll} \dfrac{\$4}{\$0.499} & \dfrac{\$4}{\$0.522} \\ = 8.016 : 1 & = 7.663 : 1 \end{array}$$

The price/earning ratio in year 2014 was 8.016: 1 and the price/earning ratio in year 2013 was 7.663: 1

Interpretation:

A high price earnings ratio shows that investors are expecting a higher earnings growth in the future compared to lower price earnings ratio.

Investors were expecting higher growth earnings in year 2015 than the earning they will be expecting in year 2014 because the P/E ratio in year 2014 was greater than the P/E ratio in year 2013.

Therefore, the P/E ratio of 8.016 in year 2014 was more favorable than P/E ratio of 7.663 calculated in year 2013.

CHAPTER SIX

Computation of Profitability Ratios

The following formulas are used to compute profitability ratio:

1. Gross Profit Margin = $\dfrac{\text{Gross Profit}}{\text{Revenue}} \times \dfrac{100}{1}$

Gross profit margin shows the efficiency with which management manufactures or sells each unit of products.

A high gross profit margin may be a symbol of good and efficient management and a low gross profit margin may reflect high cost of goods due to management's ability to purchase inventory at favorable terms.

2. Net profit margin = $\dfrac{\text{Net profit}}{\text{Revenue}} \times \dfrac{100}{1}$

The Net profit, however, can be any of these:
    i.   Net Profit before taxation (NPBT)
    ii.   Net Profit after taxation (NPAT)
    iii.   Net Profit before interest and taxation (NPBIT)

Net Profit Margin measures how effective a company is at cost control. A higher net profit margin indicates that costs are being minimized and revenues are being maximized. Net profit margin is a good standard of comparison of companies in the same industry.

3. Operating expenses ratios = $\dfrac{\text{Operating expenses}}{\text{Sales}} \times \dfrac{100}{1}$

Operating expenses comprise of distribution expenses and administrative expenses.

Higher operating expenses ratios are regarded as unfavorable because they will leave little operating income to meet up interest and dividend payments.

4. Return on Capital Employed = $\dfrac{\text{Return}}{\text{Capital employed}}$

The general formula for the calculation of Return on Capital Employed (ROCE) is mentioned above.

Return on Capital Employed is an accounting ratio that is used to measure the efficiency to which the capital of a company is used to generate profitability.

There are different formulas for the calculation of return on capital employed. However, the most important issue is to compare like with like so that there will be consistency between the numerator and the denominator.

If capital employed is defined as total assets minus current assets i.e. share capital plus Reserves plus Long-term Liabilities, then the return (Numerator) mean profit earned by all the capital. Therefore, the formula for this kind of return on capital employed is described below:

Return on Capital employed (ROCE) =

$\dfrac{\text{Net Profit before Interest and Taxation}}{\text{Shareholder's funds + Non-current liabilities}}$

A higher ROCE shows that capital is more efficiently utilized when it is compared to a lower ROCE. For example, where ROCE of two companies in the same industry are compared, the company that has higher ROCE is regarded as the company that utilizes its capital more efficiently than the company that has lower ROCE.

Return on Capital Employed (ROCE) is more appropriate for the comparison of the performance of capital intensive companies such as utilities companies and telecommunication companies.

CHAPTER SEVEN

Liquidity or Short-Term Solvency Ratio

Types of liquidity ratio are as follows:

1. Current Ratio = $\dfrac{\text{Current Assets}}{\text{Current Liability}}$

Current ratio is used to measure a company ability to meet its short-term financial obligation. Examples of short-term financial obligation are short-term loan, bank-overdraft etc.

A current ratio of greater than one means that the company has higher current assets than current liabilities.

Current ratio is not the best ratio for the measurement of liquidity of a company because it does not measure the quality of assets. For example, where the assets of a company comprises of obsolete inventory and large amount of allowance for doubtful debts, then the company ability to redeem its debt may be difficult. It is therefore, advisable that too much reliance must not be placed on current ratio.

2. Acid Test Ratio = $\dfrac{\text{Current Assets - Inventory}}{\text{Current Liabilities}}$

Acid test ratio is a more reliable ratio that can be used to evaluate the liquidity of a company. Acid test ratio is also called quick ratio.

It is generally accepted that quick ratio of 1:1 is regarded as satisfactory liquidity.

3. Cash ratio = $\dfrac{\text{Cash + Cash Equivalent}}{\text{Current Liabilities}}$

It is generally accepted that cash ratio of 1:1 is satisfactory. Too much cash should not be kept and very low cash should not be kept by a company.

A higher cash ratio is not always good because cash should not be kept idle. A very low cash ratio is not good because the company may fail to meet its short-term financial obligation as at when due.

4. Accounts Receivable Collection Period

$$= \frac{\text{Average accounts receivable}}{\text{Credit Sales}} \times \frac{365}{1}$$

Note:
Average accounts receivable
$$= \frac{\text{opening receivable} + \text{closing receivables}}{2}$$

Average receivable collection period measures the speed of collection in days. The shorter period of collection indicates efficient collection period, while a long period of collection implies a very inefficient collection power.

5. Accounts Receivable Turnover $= \dfrac{\text{Credit Sales}}{\text{Average accounts receivable}}$

Accounts receivable turnover indicates number of times debtors turnover each year. The higher the value of account receivable turnover rate, the more efficient credit is being managed by the management.

6. Accounts Payable Period $= \dfrac{\text{Average accounts payable}}{\text{Credit Purchases}} \times 365$

Accounts payable payments period measures the numbers of days in which suppliers will be paid.

7. Stock Turnover Period $= \dfrac{\text{Average inventory}}{\text{Cost of goods sold}} \times 365\text{days}$

Stock turnover period indicates the number of days that it would take a company to convert its inventory into revenue. The lower stock turnover period indicates a better management of inventory, while a higher stock turnover period indicates inefficient management of inventory.

8. Stock Turnover Rate $= \dfrac{\text{Cost of goods sold}}{\text{Average Inventory}} \times 365\text{days}$

Stock Turnover Rate is used to measure the number of times in which inventory will be sold and replaced. The higher the stock turnover rate indicates efficient performance of the inventory management team.

CHAPTER EIGHT

LONG -TERM STABILITY RATIO

Debts ratio $=$ $\dfrac{\text{Total debts}}{\text{Shareholders' funds}}$

Debt ratio reflects the extent to which debt financing has been used in the business.

Gearing ratio $=$ $\dfrac{\text{Prior Charge capital}}{\text{Total Capital}}$

Gearing ratio is a ratio that is used to measure the proportion of debt to total financing.

The prior charge capital is the capital having the right to fixed income. Examples of such capital are:

i.	Debentures
ii.	Preferred stock
iii.	Long-term loan

The total capital consists of the following:

i.	Common stocks
ii.	Reserves
iii.	Prior charge capital
iv.	Minority interest (in group situation)

CHAPTER NINE

LIMITATIONS OF FINANCIAL RATIOS

There are some limitations to financial ratios. The following are the limitations to financial ratios:

i. Financial ratios can only be used to compare the results of company having the same accounting policies. Financial ratio cannot be used to compare companies that have different accounting policies, otherwise wrong decisions would be taken by the users of accounting information.

ii. If effect of inflation is not considered in the calculation of financial ratio, misleading result will be arrived at.

iii. There is no stable standard that can be laid down for a perfect ratio.

iv. Financial ratio can only create an avenue for further investigation. It is not sufficient enough to make absolute final decision.

REFERENCES

Toye Adelaja (2015) – Basic Financial Accounting (MCQ & A)

www.accoutninghour.com

ICAN Study Pack (FA II)